Voice of Witness Student Workbook:

Oral Histories
of Displacement and Determination

Soledad Castillo
From *Solito, Solita: Crossing Borders with Youth Refugees from Central America*
Edited by Steven Mayers and Jonathan Freedman

Mohammed "Mike" Ali
From *Six by Ten: Stories from Solitary*
Edited by Taylor Pendergrass and Mateo Hoke

Voice of Witness (VOW) is an oral history nonprofit that advances human rights by amplifying the voices of people impacted by—and fighting against—injustice. VOW's work is driven by the transformative power of the story, and by a strong belief that an understanding of systemic injustice is incomplete without deep listening and learning from people with firsthand experience. Through our oral history book series and education program, we amplify unheard voices, teach ethics-driven storytelling, and partner with human rights advocates. *www.voiceofwitness.org*

Workbook design by Ragina Johnson.
Narrative portrait illustrations by Christine Shields.

ISBN: 979-8-218-23706-6

Dear Teachers,

This Voice of Witness Student Workbook is designed to introduce your students to oral history narratives in an immersive, interactive way. We hope your students will use this workbook to reflect, make connections, generate questions, and create their own unique responses.

Each story in this book began as much longer in-person conversations with our narrators, Soledad Castillo and Muhammad "Mike" Ali. We encourage you to point out to your students that even though these stories read like a book, they actually come from the voices of the real people who lived them. We hope students will see that everyone has a story to tell and, as we like to say at Voice of Witness, *if you can speak it, you can write it!*

After completing this workbook with your students, you can explore the many wide-ranging applications for using oral history in the classroom. Largely, oral histories humanize history and provide meaningful counternarratives to the "single stories" that pervade dominant media. Many of the oral history narratives in the Voice of Witness book series fit perfectly into larger units that focus on identity and community, migration and displacement, systems of power and oppression, or action and resistance. In addition, students can participate in the oral history process themselves. In conducting and editing oral history interviews, students learn to meaningfully engage with their community with curiosity and empathetic listening.

More oral history resources can be found on the Voice of Witness website, linked at the end of this workbook. We have created additional lesson plans to accompany the narratives in this workbook, as well as information on how to create your own oral history unit.

Dear Students,

This workbook contains two oral histories from Soledad Castillo and Muhammad "Mike" Ali, who shared their stories with us in a series of interviews. Oral history is a way of capturing people's stories and learning about history through the first-hand experiences of people who lived it. Oral history lets us listen to someone tell their story in their own words, giving us an opportunity to see the world through different perspectives.

In the first story, Soledad shares her journey as a young refugee from Honduras, building a new life in the United States, and pursuing her dreams despite the challenges she faced. In the second story, Mike tells us about how his childhood shaped his choices, his experience with incarceration and immigration detention, and the importance of his family over everything.

While Soledad and Mike talk about the difficult, stressful, painful, and scary parts of their lives, there are also moments of strength, determination, success, and hope. Oral history gives us the space to see a person's life as more than just one single event, whether that's their worst or best moment. By reading and listening to these oral histories, we can see people like Soledad and Mike as more than a stereotype or statistic; they are whole human beings with complicated stories, and there are many more people around us waiting to tell their stories too.

As you read Soledad and Mike's stories in this workbook, we hope you'll fill the pages with your own thoughts and ideas. You'll find sections for reflection and activities to finish, but don't be afraid to highlight your favorite quotes, draw how you're feeling, circle what feels important to you, and find space to insert yourself! This is your workbook now. Hold these stories in your hands, and don't forget that your own stories are worth sharing.

dad

At the time of this interview, Soledad Castillo was a college student at the City College of San Francisco. Soledad was born in Honduras and lived there until the age of 14, when she crossed the border into the United States with her father. As a girl, Soledad was subjected to multiple instances of physical and sexual abuse, neglect, and abandonment. Through her own will and the help of others, she has been able to both succeed in college and engage in legislative reforms to help other migrant children in the foster care system.

Life In Honduras

My mother had her first baby, my older sister, Angela, when she was about sixteen, and she was about nineteen when she had me. I was born on June 6, 1992, in Tegucigalpa, Honduras. My parents broke up before I was born and they lived apart. We were really poor, the poorest family in our little neighborhood. My father left for the United States when I was five. My mother got together with Faustino, the man who would become my stepfather. My mother was scared of him, because he drank a lot and was a violent guy. He used to hit my mom and throw chairs at her. He never had a stable job. My mom was really weak and never stood up for me. She let other people make decisions for her.

One day when I was twelve, my mom left me with my stepfather and his daughters. Faustino got drunk that night, and he came over to my bed and touched me. I ran barefoot up the hill to his parents' house, crying, screaming, and asking for help. When my mom got there the next day, I was scared. I didn't know what she would say. I told her about what Faustino had done to me, but she didn't believe me. She tried to hit me. She sent me to another part of the city to work for relatives of my stepfather. I was their servant. They didn't pay me, but they gave me food to eat. I was only twelve.

When I was about to turn fourteen, my father decided to return to Honduras to see me. I waited by the door for him, wondering, *What will he look like? How will I feel after all these years?* My dad came in a car, and when he got out, I went and hugged him. He's really short, like me. He cried when he saw me. I just felt happy. But I was mad at him because he had left me alone, you know? When my stepfather abused me, my father wasn't there for me. But after seeing him, I started feeling something for him.

*Al momento de esta entrevista, Soledad Castillo era
una estudiante universitaria en el City College de San
Francisco. Soledad nació en Honduras y vivió allí hasta
los 14 años cuando cruzó la frontera de Estados Unidos
con su papá. Cuando era niña, Soledad estuvo sujeta
a múltiples instancias de abuso físico y sexual,
negligencia y abandono. Por su propia voluntad y la
ayuda de otras personas, ha podido tener éxito en la
universidad y participar en reformas legislativas para
ayudar a otros niños inmigrantes en el sistema de
acogida conocido como "foster care".*

La Vida En Honduras

Mi madre tuvo a su primer bebé, mi hermana mayor, Ángela, cuando tenía unos
dieciséis años, y ella tenía unos diecinueve años cuando me tuvo a mí. Nací el 6
de junio de 1992 en Tegucigalpa, Honduras. Antes de que yo naciera, mis papás
ya se habían separado y vivían por separado. Éramos muy pobres, la familia más
pobre de nuestro pequeño barrio. Mi padre se fue a Estados Unidos cuando yo
tenía cinco años. Mi madre se juntó con Faustino, el hombre que se convertiría
en mi padrastro. Mi madre le tenía miedo, porque él tomaba mucho y era un
tipo violento. Solía golpear a mi madre y tirarle sillas. Él nunca tuvo un trabajo
estable. Mi madre era muy débil y nunca me defendía. Ella dejaba que otras
personas tomaran decisiones por ella.

Un día, cuando tenía doce años, mi madre me dejó con mi padrastro y sus
hijas. Esa noche, Faustino se emborrachó, se acercó a mi cama y me tocó. Corrí
descalza colina arriba hasta la casa de sus padres, llorando, gritando y pidiendo
ayuda. Al día siguiente, cuando mi mamá llegó, tenía miedo. No sabía lo que
ella diría. Le conté lo que Faustino me había hecho, pero no me creyó. Intentó
pegarme. Me mandó a otra parte de la ciudad para trabajar para unos familiares
de mi padrastro. Yo era su sirvienta. No me pagaban, pero me daban de comer.
Yo tenía apenas doce años.

Cuando estaba a punto de cumplir catorce años, mi padre decidió volver a
Honduras para verme. Lo esperé junto a la puerta y pensaba, *¿Qué aspecto
tendrá? ¿Cómo me sentiré después de todos estos años?* Mi papá llegó en un
carro y, cuando se bajó, fui a abrazarlo. Él es muy bajito, como yo. Y lloró cuando
me vio. Yo simplemente me sentía feliz. Pero estaba enojada con él porque me

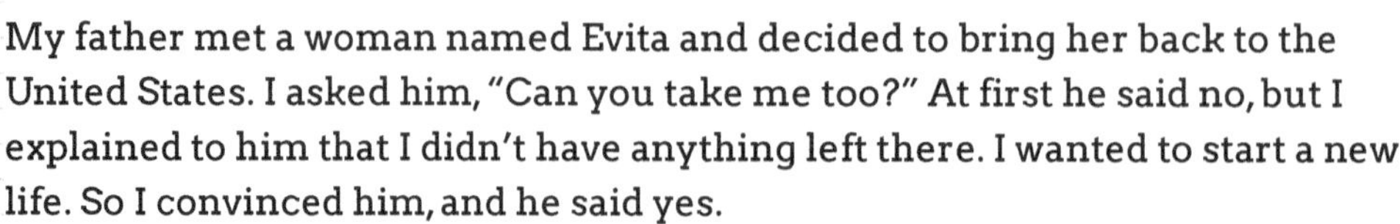

My father met a woman named Evita and decided to bring her back to the United States. I asked him, "Can you take me too?" At first he said no, but I explained to him that I didn't have anything left there. I wanted to start a new life. So I convinced him, and he said yes.

Coming To America

It took more than one month to get to the United States. The three of us left Honduras and went to Guatemala on the bus. There were gangsters on board. First, one guy took out a gun, and then the other guys did too. They put a gun to my head, telling me to give them all my money. I didn't have money, but they didn't believe me. They took my pants off. I don't remember their faces. I just remember their hands. I remember hands touching me all over my body, and I couldn't say anything. At that time, I was fourteen.

Making Connections

Name one other person who has overcome many challenges and hardships to get to where they are today

The gangsters took money from my father, so we didn't have enough money to eat for the rest of the trip. We stayed in Guatemala for one day and then got in a van to go to Mexico. We went from van to van. We had to lie down with many people, one on top of the other. The *coyotes* put cardboard on top of us so *La Migra* wouldn't see us if they pulled us over. It was hard to breathe, and we didn't eat either. They didn't want to stop.

Finally, we reached a house, somewhere in Texas, a really nice place. A guy with his wife and their little daughter lived there, and they spoke Spanish. We were really hungry, and they gave us food. They just told us, "Don't go outside." After that, someone came in a van to take us from Texas to Sacramento. It was a long trip. They stopped to pick up other people at different houses, and the police stopped us twice. There was a hiding place under the floor where they put people in the van. There were air holes, but there were too many people. I was next to my father, and we were holding our arms in and we were curled up, and it was

había dejado sola, ¿cierto? Cuando mi padrastro abusó de mí, mi papá no estuvo a mi lado. Pero después de verlo, comencé a sentir algo por él.

Mi papá conoció a una mujer, Evita, y decidió llevársela con él a los Estados Unidos. Yo le pregunté, "¿Puede llevarme a mí también?" Al principio dijo que no, pero le expliqué que a mí no me quedaba nada en Honduras. Yo quería comenzar una nueva vida. Así que lo convencí, y él dijo que sí.

El Viaje A Los Estados Unidos

Nos tomó más de un mes llegar a los Estados Unidos. Los tres salimos de Honduras y nos fuimos a Guatemala en bus. Había pandilleros a bordo. Primero, un muchacho sacó un arma, y luego los demás también. Me pusieron un arma en la cabeza y me decían que les diera todo mi dinero. Yo no tenía dinero, pero no me creían. Me quitaron los pantalones. No recuerdo sus caras. Sólo recuerdo sus manos. Recuerdo las manos tocándome todo el cuerpo y yo no podía decir nada. Yo tenía catorce años en ese momento.

Los pandilleros le quitaron dinero a mi papá, así que no tuvimos suficiente dinero para comer durante el resto del viaje. Nos quedamos un día en Guatemala y después nos subimos a una camioneta para ir a México. Íbamos de camioneta en camioneta. Teníamos que ir acostados con muchas personas, íbamos unos encima de otros. Los coyotes nos pusieron cartón encima para que si la Migra nos paraba, no nos pudieran ver. Era difícil respirar y tampoco comimos nada. Ellos no quisieron parar.

Al fin llegamos a una casa en algún lugar en Texas. Era un lugar muy bonito. Ahí vivía un señor con su esposa y su hijita, y hablaban español. Teníamos mucha hambre y ellos nos dieron comida. Solo nos dijeron, "No vayan a salir". Después de eso, alguien llegó en una camioneta para llevarnos de Texas a Sacramento. Fue un viaje largo. Pararon para recoger a otras personas de diferentes casas y la policía nos paró dos veces. Había un escondite debajo del piso de la camioneta, ahí metían a la gente. Había agujeros para que el aire entrara, pero eran demasiadas personas. Yo estaba al lado de mi papá, íbamos con los brazos pegados al cuerpo y enrollados, era realmente difícil respirar. Tuvimos que permanecer callados todo el tramo. Nos decían, "Ahí viene la policía. ¡Cállense, cállense!"

really hard to breathe. We had to stay quiet the whole time. They'd say, "Here come the police. Stay quiet, stay quiet!"

Life In California

We got to Hayward, California, where my father lived. It seemed really fancy. I looked at the glass buildings, and I was like, *Wow!* I was happy, but at the same time I felt scared and weird because I had never lived with my dad or known his family. I asked him, "Can I go to school?" and he said, "No school, you have to work!"

We went to the Mission District in San Francisco, and I got fake papers that said I was twenty-one, even though I was really fourteen. Then I started working at a laundry shop in Hayward. I felt lonely because my father had fallen in love with Evita, and he forgot about me. He started telling me, "You have to pay me back for the trip." To pay my father back, I began working two shifts a day at the laundry service. I started at seven in the morning and I got out at one the next morning. I'd sleep for four hours. When my check came, I didn't even see it. My dad would just take it.

Making Connections

Highlight an assumption that some Americans make about people who immigrate to the US.

One day, someone invited Evita to San Francisco. She told me to come too. We went to the Embarcadero in San Francisco, on Pier 39. There were two guys there, and she started kissing one of them. She said to the other guy, "You can kiss her," meaning me. Later, I told my dad about it, but he wouldn't believe me because he was in love with her. He hit me on the back with a belt. I don't know why. That was a stupid reason to get mad at me. I cried, "Why do you have to believe everything she says? She doesn't love you. It's just for the money." Then he got really mad.

I felt so frustrated, and I said, "I'm really thankful for you helping me, but you don't have to hit me. You don't even know me well!" That same night, I ran

La Vida En California

Llegamos a Hayward, California, donde vivía mi papá. Parecía un área muy elegante. Miré los edificios de vidrio y pensé, "¡Guau!" Estaba feliz, pero al mismo tiempo, me sentía asustada y extraña porque nunca había vivido con mi papá ni conocía a su familia. Le pregunté, "¿Puedo ir a la escuela?" y me dijo, "¡Nada de escuela, tenés que trabajar!".

Fuimos al Distrito de Misión en San Francisco y conseguí papeles falsos que decían que yo tenía veintiún años, aunque en realidad tenía catorce. Luego, empecé a trabajar en una lavandería en Hayward. Me sentía sola porque mi papá se había enamorado de Evita y se había olvidado de mí. Empezó a decirme, "Tenés que pagarme el viaje". Para pagarle a mi papá, empecé a trabajar dos turnos al día en la lavandería. Empezaba a las siete de la mañana y salía a la una de la madrugada el día siguiente. Dormí cuatro horas. Cuando llegaba mi cheque, ni lo veía. Mi papá lo agarraba.

Un día, alguien invitó a Evita a San Francisco. Me dijo que fuera con ella. Fuimos al Embarcadero de San Francisco, al Pier 39. Había dos muchachos y ella empezó a besar a uno de ellos. Y le dijo al otro, "Puedes besarla", refiriéndose a mí. Más tarde, yo se lo conté a mi papá, pero no me creyó porque estaba enamorado de ella. Entonces, me pegó en la espalda con un cinturón. No sé por qué. Era una razón estúpida para enojarse conmigo. Grité, "¿Por qué tiene que creer todo lo que ella dice? Ella no lo ama. Es sólo por el dinero". Entonces, se enojó mucho.

Me sentí tan frustrada y le dije, "Estoy muy agradecida de que me haya ayudado, pero no tiene que pegarme. ¡Ni siquiera me conoce bien!" Esa misma noche, me escapé. Mi papá fue a buscarme. Pensó que yo estaba jugando, que era una broma. Por teléfono le dije que no, que no quería verlo más. Él me había dejado marcas en el cuerpo. Me dijo que yo había herido sus sentimientos, porque él me había traído a Estados Unidos. Yo le dije, "Si vuelve a venir a la casa, voy a llamar a la policía".

Después de eso, me sentí muy sola. No tenía a nadie. Seguía trabajando mucho, pagándole a mi papá y enviándole dinero a mi madre. Ese verano, un muchacho que era amigo de mi amigo, empezó a hablarme. Él era mayor, tenía como veinticinco años. Yo solo tenía quince años. Se llamaba Sergio. Era muy romántico y venía a mi trabajo y me traía flores. Y yo le di todo de mí; estaba tan desesperada por encontrar a alguien que me quisiera y se preocupara por mí. Empezamos una relación en julio. Él tenía un viaje a México en agosto o septiembre. Antes de irse, me dijo, "Volveré por ti".

away. My father went looking for me. He thought that I was kidding, that it was a prank. On the phone I told him no, I didn't want to see him anymore. He'd left marks on my body. He said I hurt his feelings, because he brought me to the United States. I told him, "If you come to the house again, I will call the police."

Stop To Think...

Why do you think Soledad wanted to leave Honduras?

So after that, I felt really alone. I didn't have anyone. I was still working a lot, paying back my father and sending money to my mom. That summer, this guy, a friend of my friend, started talking to me. He was older, like twenty-five. I was only fifteen. His name was Sergio. He was very romantic and would come to my job and bring me flowers. I gave him all of myself; I was so desperate to find someone to love and care about me. We started a relationship in July. He had plans to go to Mexico in August or September. Before leaving, he said, "I'll come back for you."

After he left, I tried to call him. The first time he answered, the second time he answered, but after one week, he stopped answering. I discovered that he had gotten married in Mexico. That took everything from me. I went into a depression and lost my job. I didn't want to work or eat.

A friend from work saw my condition and said, "Do you want help?" I said, "Yeah, I want to be far away. Bring me to an orphanage. Bring me somewhere." She took me to San Francisco Human Services. I told the counselor my story—that I was here alone. Then these people—I think they were from child protection—took me to an office here in San Francisco. The next day they said, "We have a family for you." I didn't know why, because I didn't need a family. They said, "You will be put into the foster care system."

So they took me to a house in Rohnert Park. It was dark, with a lot of masks and deer heads on the walls. The foster woman was from Mexico and she was kind of old. The social worker introduced us. The foster mom said, "Go to your room," and that was it. The first day, she treated me well, gave me food, but after

Después de que se fue, traté de llamarlo. La primera vez contestó, la segunda también, pero al cabo de una semana dejó de contestarme. Descubrí que se había casado en México. Eso me destruyó por completo. Caí en una depresión y perdí mi trabajo. No quería trabajar ni comer.

Una amiga del trabajo vio mi estado y me preguntó, "¿Quieres ayuda?". Le dije, "Sí, quiero estar lejos de aquí. Llévame a un orfanato. Llévame a algún lugar". Ella me llevó a Servicios Humanos de San Francisco. Le conté al consejero mi historia: que yo estaba aquí sola. Entonces estas personas— creo que eran de protección de menores—me llevaron a una oficina aquí en San Francisco. Al día siguiente me dijeron: "Tenemos una familia para ti". No sabía por qué, porque yo no necesitaba una familia. Me dijeron, "Te pondrán en el sistema de acogida".

Así que me llevaron a una casa en Rohnert Park. Era oscura, con muchas máscaras y cabezas de venado en las paredes. La mujer de acogida era de México y era algo mayor. La trabajadora social nos presentó. La mamá de acogida solo me dijo, "Vete a tu habitación". El primer día me trató bien, me dio comida, pero después apenas me daba una nada de comer. Me obligó a limpiar la casa. Me puso en la escuela de verano y me desmayé tres veces en la escuela porque me estaba muriendo de hambre.

Otra muchacha de acogida, de San Francisco, vino a la casa. Se llamaba Julia y ella vio cómo me trataban. Hablaba inglés y había nacido aquí, así que dijo, "No, esto no está bien, Soledad". Le dijo a la trabajadora social, "Tienes que hablar con Soledad". Al final, la trabajadora social me llevó al lado y ahí le dije que no comía, que la mamá de acogida ni siquiera le daba de comer a los bebés que cuidaba. La trabajadora social puso cara de sorpresa y dijo, "No vamos a llevarte de regreso allá". Nunca regresé a esa casa. Me recogió del hospital y me llevó a Cloverdale a vivir con una nueva familia.

Mis nuevos padres de acogida me recibieron con flores y me sentí bienvenida. Tenían tres niños, una casa linda y eran personas de México, muy cálidas, limpias y educadas. Su hija había muerto cuando tenía un año y hubiera tenido mi misma edad. Lucy, la nueva madre de acogida, era amable y tuvimos una buena relación. Me sentía parte de la familia que siempre había soñado tener.

that, she barely gave me anything to eat. She made me clean the house.
She put me in summer school, and I passed out three times in school because I
was starving.

Another foster girl from San Francisco came to the house. Her name was Julia,
and she saw the way that they were treating me. She spoke English and was
born here, so she said, "No, this isn't right, Soledad." She told her social worker,
"You need to talk with Soledad." So finally the social worker took me aside, and I
told her that I don't eat, that the foster mom doesn't even give food to the babies
she's taking care of. The social worker looked surprised and said, "We're not
taking you back there." I never went back to that house. She picked me up from
the hospital and brought me to Cloverdale to live with a new family.

My new foster parents greeted me with flowers, and I felt welcome. They had
three boys, a nice house, and were really warm, clean, educated people from
Mexico. Their daughter had died at age one and would've been the same age as
me. Lucy, the new foster mom, was nice and I had a good relationship with her. I
felt like I was in the family that I always dreamed about having.

They put me in a new school. I had two excellent teachers who encouraged me.
I started learning English and worked hard. My new social worker was more
proactive, assigning a personal tutor who helped me pass all my classes. My
foster parents were proud of me, and always said, "This is my daughter," when
introducing me.

Stop To Think...

**Write three words that describe this part of
Soledad's story.**

Becoming An Independent Adult

When I turned eighteen, my foster parents told me, "Now you're eighteen.
You're independent." After two months of paying them rent, I made the
decision to move to San Francisco. I had the option to stay with them, and to
pay them rent and everything. I liked it there, but there wasn't enough for me.

Me pusieron en una nueva escuela. Tuve dos maestros excelentes que me animaban. Comencé a aprender inglés y a estudiar mucho. Mi nueva trabajadora social fue más proactiva y me asignó un tutor personal que me ayudó a aprobar todas las clases. Mis padres de acogida estaban orgullosos de mí y siempre que me presentaban, decían, "Esta es mi hija".

Convirtiéndome En Una Adulta Independiente

Cuando cumplí dieciocho años, mis padres de acogida me dijeron, "Ahora tienes dieciocho años. Eres independiente". Después de dos meses de pagarles la renta, tomé la decisión de mudarme a San Francisco. Tenía la opción de quedarme con ellos, pagándoles la renta y todo lo demás. Me gustaba estar ahí, pero no había suficiente para mi. No había suficientes empleos porque era un pueblo chiquito. Así que les dije que asistiría al community college, seguiría adelante, encontraría mi propio lugar para vivir y obtendría mi GED.

Estaban muy tristes y lloraron. Éramos muy unidos, así que fue duro. Tenía una familia, me preparaban la comida, me ayudaban con todo; me trataban como a una princesa con todos los beneficios.

Me vine a San Francisco en agosto de 2011. Regresar sola a San Francisco fue difícil, especialmente la primera semana. Hay un programa llamado Larkin Street que ayuda a jóvenes que han estado en el servicio de acogida. Mi trabajadora social me puso en contacto con ellos y me dieron un contrato de renta de dos años en un lugar llamado Holloway House.

Rick, el director de Holloway House, me ayudó a inscribirme en City College. En la secundaria, sólo escribía un ensayo al año. Al venir al City College, tenía que hacer un ensayo cada dos o tres semanas, una gran diferencia. El profesor era muy difícil. Lloré muchas veces. Decía, "¡No sé cómo hacerlo!" Y el maestro me decía, "Vuelve a intentarlo". Reescribía los ensayos como tres veces. En aquel momento no conocía a ningún tutor. Trabajaba sola. Al final saqué una A en esa clase y B en las demás.

Tenía veinte años cuando me fui de Holloway House, después de casi dos años de vivir ahí. Me mudé a un cuarto cercano. La renta era de 600 dólares al mes. Tenía un trabajo de tiempo completo pero vivía en malas condiciones. Había ratas y contraje una enfermedad de la piel porque estaba muy sucio ahí. Decidí pedir ayuda a Guardian Scholars, un grupo de apoyo para jóvenes en acogida, para encontrar otro lugar. Me dijeron, "Hay una oportunidad en un edificio nuevo en la Ocean Avenue, así que presentemos una solicitud y veamos". Tenía que escribir una carta de presentación y mostrar mis ingresos y promedio

There weren't enough jobs, because it was a little town. So I told them that I would go to community college, move on, and find my own place, get my GED.

They were really sad; they cried. We were really close so it was hard. I had a family, and my food was prepared, everything; I was treated like a princess with all the benefits.

I came to San Francisco in August 2011. Coming back to San Francisco by myself was hard, especially the first week. There's a program called Larkin Street for former foster youth. My social worker connected me, and they put me on a lease for two years at a place called Holloway House.

Rick, the manager at Holloway House, helped me enroll at City College. In high school, I'd only written like one essay a year. Coming to City College, I had to do an essay every two or three weeks—a big difference. The teacher was really tough. I cried many times. I'd say, "I don't know how to do it!" And my teacher would say, "Just try again." I would rewrite the essays like three times. I didn't know any tutors then. I just worked by myself. I eventually got an A in the class, and B's in the others.

I left Holloway House after almost two years, when I was twenty. I moved to a room nearby. The rent was $600 a month. I was working full time but living in bad conditions. There were rats, and I got a skin disease because it was so dirty. I decided to ask Guardian Scholars, a support group for foster youth, to help me find another place. They told me, "There is an opportunity in a new building on Ocean Avenue, so let's apply and see." I had to write a statement and show my income and GPA. There was stiff competition, because there were hundreds of applicants, but I was the only one with a 3.0 GPA.

I was selected! This apartment is brand new, awesome! I always dreamed of having a kitchen, because I like to cook. It has a nice table to eat on, a big refrigerator, and a really big bathroom. It's clean, quiet, close to the college and Whole Foods. There's a beautiful view outside the window. And it's safe because they have a guard downstairs twenty four hours a day.

Future Plans

My dream for the future is to graduate from City College, and that dream is very close. I will get an associate degree in sociology and social science in spring 2016, after being in college for three years. I'm getting a certificate in Latino Studies this summer. My next step is to transfer to a university, graduate

de calificaciones (GPA, por sus siglas en inglés). Hubo una dura competencia, porque había cientos de solicitantes, pero yo era la única con un GPA de 3.0.

¡Fui seleccionada! ¡Este apartamento era nuevo e increíble! Siempre soñé con tener una cocina, porque me gusta cocinar. Tiene una bonita mesa para comer, un refrigerador grande y un baño bien espacioso. Es limpio, tranquilo, cerca de la universidad y del supermercado Whole Foods. Tiene una hermosa vista desde la ventana. Y es seguro porque tiene un guardia abajo las veinticuatro horas del día.

Los Planes Para El Futuro

Mi sueño para el futuro es graduarme del City College y ese sueño está muy cerca. Obtendré un título de asociada en sociología y ciencias sociales en la primavera de 2016, después de haber estado tres años en la universidad. Este verano obtendré un certificado en Estudios Latinoamericanos. Mi próximo paso es transferirme a una universidad, graduarme con una licenciatura en sociología y encontrar un mejor trabajo. Ahorita, estoy haciendo mi pasantía trabajando con jóvenes de acogida, intentando cambiar las cosas para que otros jóvenes no tengan las mismas malas experiencias que yo tuve.

Trabajo con California Youth Connection, una organización que trabaja para cambiar políticas. He ido a Sacramento a hablar con los legisladores estatales. Por ejemplo, al principio no sabía lo que significaba estar en foster care. Creo que los trabajadores sociales deben informar a los jóvenes de lo que pueden esperar y de los servicios que están disponibles. Otro problema es que si una joven en el sistema de acogida queda embarazada, le quitan al bebé y también lo ponen en foster care. Intentamos cambiar el sistema para que las madres y sus bebés no vayan con familias distintas. Si soy una persona joven en el sistema de acogida, no quiero que mi bebé tenga la misma vida que yo tuve.

Por eso vine a este país. Por eso caminé por el desierto durante días. Todos los retos por los que he pasado han valido la pena. Muchos estadounidenses piensan que venimos aquí a quitarles el trabajo, a hacer cosas malas, a aprovecharnos del país. No soy una persona mala. Vine aquí para sobrevivir, para tener una mejor vida en este mundo, para ayudar a mi familia y a otras personas. No había forma de sobrevivir en mi tierra natal. No elegí venir aquí. No tuve otra opción. Quiero que el presidente de los Estados Unidos vea que no venimos a hacer nada malo. Venimos aquí para educarnos y tener una vida mejor.

with a bachelor's degree in sociology, and find a better job. Right now, I have an internship working with foster youth, trying to make change, so the same bad experiences that I had do not happen to other youth.

I'm working with California Youth Connection, an organization that works on changing policy. I've been going to Sacramento to talk to state legislators. For example, in the beginning I didn't know what it meant to be in foster care. I think social workers should tell the youth what they can expect and what services are available. Another problem is that if a foster youth gets pregnant, they take the baby away and put it in the foster system as well. We're trying to change the system so mothers and babies don't go with different families. If I'm a foster youth, I don't want my baby to have the same life I had.

Interview Skills

What is one thing you would want to ask Soledad about her journey from Honduras to the United States?

This is why I came to this country. This is why I walked for days in the desert. All the struggles that I've been through have been worth it. Many Americans think that we come here to take their jobs, to do bad things, to take advantage of the country. I'm not a bad person. I came here to survive, to do better in this world, to help my family and other people. There was no way to survive in my homeland. I didn't choose to come here. I didn't have another option. I want the president of the United States to see that we are not coming here to do anything bad. We come here to get educated and have a better life.

It's exciting to know that other people will read my story. I believe that telling one's story is a way to healing. Sharing my own story has changed my life. Every time I'm sad or I feel like giving up, I read my story and think, *Wow, look at all the things that have come true! I can do it! This is only a bad day, a bad week. I can get up and continue my life.*

Es emocionante saber que otras personas leerán mi historia. Creo que contar nuestras historias es una manera de sanar. Compartir mi propia historia me ha cambiado la vida. Cada vez que estoy triste o tengo ganas de rendirme, leo mi historia y pienso, "¡Híjole, mira todas las cosas que se han hecho realidad! ¡Puedo hacerlo! Este es solamente un mal día, una mala semana. Puedo levantarme y seguir con mi vida".

In each of the four boxes below, draw a picture that represents an important part of Soledad's journey. Use labels, captions, and/or speech bubbles to help you capture who is in your drawing, what is happening, and where it takes place. Use colors and symbols to help you capture how each person is feeling in that moment. Don't worry if you don't consider yourself to be a great artist—just try your best!

Use an excerpt from Soledad's story to create your own blackout poem! Pick out the most important words and phrases in the excerpt, then use a marker to black out everything else. Use the words that are left over to create a poem: you can change the order of the words, and add line breaks or punctuation wherever you want. The only trick is that you cannot add any new words!

Excerpt:

When I was about to turn fourteen, my father decided to return to Honduras to see me. I waited by the door for him, wondering, What will he look like? How will I feel after all these years? My dad came in a car, and when he got out, I went and hugged him. He's really short, like me. He cried when he saw me. I just felt happy. But I was mad at him because he had left me alone, you know? When my stepfather abused me, my father wasn't there for me. But after seeing him, I started feeling something for him.

With Blackouts:

Finished Poem:

I was fourteen.
I waited by the door,
Wondering.
Years came in a car,
Short, happy.
But I was mad,
Alone:
Seeing,
Feeling something.

Excerpt:

We stayed in Guatemala for one day and then got in a van to go to Mexico. We went from van to van. We had to lie down with many people, one on top of the other. The coyotes put cardboard on top of us so La Migra wouldn't see us if they pulled us over. It was hard to breathe, and we didn't eat either. They didn't want to stop. Finally, we reached a house, somewhere in Texas, a really nice place. A guy with his wife and their little daughter lived there, and they spoke Spanish. We were really hungry, and they gave us food. They just told us, "Don't go outside." After that, someone came in a van to take us from Texas to Sacramento. It was a long trip. They stopped to pick up other people at different houses, and the police stopped us twice. There was a hiding place under the floor where they put people in the van. There were air holes, but there were too many people. I was next to my father, and we were holding our arms in and we were curled up, and it was really hard to breathe. We had to stay quiet the whole time. They'd say, "Here come the police. Stay quiet, stay quiet!"

Finished Poem:

If you had a chance to write a letter to Soledad, what would you want to say? In the space provided, write a letter addressed to Soledad about your response to her story. You can ask questions, make personal connections to your own experiences, talk about what her story has taught you, express gratitude or admiration—whatever feels most important to you! Make sure to reference at least two specific details from Soledad's story in your letter.

Spend some time thinking about each of the following questions. Use the boxes provided to jot down your thoughts and to collect evidence to support your answers. Then, you will use your notes to participate in a class discussion on these questions.

What are Soledad's reasons for wanting to leave Honduras to come to the United States?

➤ Your Response:

➤ Evidence:

Do you think Soledad's expectations for what life would be like in America matched her reality? Why or why not?

➤ Your Response:

➤ Evidence:

Who or what provides support to Soledad throughout her journey of becoming an independent adult in the US?

➤ Your Response:

➤ Evidence:

Why is Soledad's dream for the future to graduate from college? What does she hope to do with her education?

➤ Your Response:

➤ Evidence:

In your opinion, what sources of support should exist for migrant youth coming to the US to seek a better life?

➤ Your Response:

How does Soledad's story challenge negative stereotypes or dominant narratives about immigrants?

➤ Your Response:

Mohammad "Mike" Ali was born in Fiji and came to the United States with his family as a child. He was initiated into gang life in the 1990s as protection from being bullied in school. He spent much of his teens and early twenties between juvenile hall, jail, and prison before being detained for deportation at age twenty-four. Mike experienced long stretches of isolation in a privately run immigration detention center and struggled to maintain hope with an uncertain sentence and the threat of deportation hanging over his head for over four years. Mike now lives with his family, working and raising four children.

Early Life

I was born in 1978 in Fiji, in a little village called Navo Nadi, and I grew up there until I was ten, in '89. That's when we came to the US. We landed in San Francisco—me, my big brother, two sisters, and my mom and dad. We had our green cards already. We came as permanent residents and were sponsored by an aunt. My mom's family was here, which is why we ended up coming here. I think we would have had a better life in Fiji.

We lived in Oakland for a year, then we moved to Hayward. My mom worked as a housekeeper and my dad was a chef. In Hayward we were the minorities. Me and my sister were the only Fijis in the whole elementary school. We got bullied a lot. The majority of kids were Mexicans. There were Blacks, whites. The Mexicans didn't like us and were always bullying us 'cause back then we didn't know about deodorant. In our houses we were cooking with a lot of curry, so we all smelled like that. They used to jump us, so me and my four homeboys, we made our own gang and we started beating them up too. We were like twelve years old and we were all Fijis, all from South Hayward. We didn't have no outsiders. Four or five guys would hit us, but then we'd grab one and beat the shit out of him. And then things just kept on escalating.

After that, me and my homeboys were just gangbanging. I was gangbanging all the way out. It was like the coolest thing to do. If you were a gangster, you were the coolest cat in the street, in school, everything. I first went to juvenile hall in '92. I pulled a gun on somebody at school. We got into it, and I happened to have a gun on me I got from one of my homeboys. But I didn't know how to use

Mohammad "Mike" Ali nació en Fiji y vino a los Estados Unidos con su familia cuando era un niño. Fue iniciado en la vida de pandillas en la década de 1990, como una protección contra el acoso escolar o el "bullying". Pasó gran parte de su adolescencia y principios de sus veinte entre el centro de detención juvenil, la cárcel y la prisión antes de ser detenido para su deportación a la edad de veinticuatro años. Mike experimentó largos períodos de aislamiento en un centro de detención de inmigrantes de gestión privada y luchó por mantener la esperanza teniendo una sentencia incierta y la amenaza de deportación sobre sus hombros durante más de cuatro años. Mike ahora vive con su familia, trabaja y cría a cuatro hijos.

Adolescencia

Nací en 1978 en Fiji, en un pequeño pueblo llamado Navo Nadi, y viví ahí hasta 1989, cuando yo tenía diez años. Fue entonces cuando nos vinimos a los Estados Unidos. Aterrizamos en San Francisco: yo, mi hermano mayor, dos hermanas y mi mamá y papá. Ya teníamos nuestras *green cards*. Vinimos como residentes permanentes y fuimos patrocinados por una tía. La familia de mi mamá estaba aquí, por eso terminamos viniendo aquí. Creo que habríamos tenido una vida mejor en Fiji.

Vivimos en Oakland durante un año, luego nos mudamos a Hayward. Mi mamá trabajaba como trabajadora de hogar y mi papá era chef. En Hayward éramos la minoría. Mi hermana y yo éramos los únicos fiyianos en toda la escuela primaria. Nos hacían mucho *bullying*. La mayoría de los niños eran mexicanos. También había estudiantes negros y blancos. A los mexicanos no les caíamos bien y siempre nos molestaban porque en ese entonces no sabíamos qué era el desodorante. En nuestras casas cocinábamos con mucho curri, así que todos olíamos a eso. Solían golpearnos, así que yo y mis cuatro *homeboys* formamos nuestra propia pandilla y empezamos a golpearlos también. Teníamos como doce años y todos éramos fiyianos, todos de South Hayward. No incorporábamos a ningún extraño. Cuatro o cinco tipos nos golpeaban, pero luego agarrábamos a uno y le dábamos una golpiza. Y luego las cosas siguieron poniéndose más rudas.

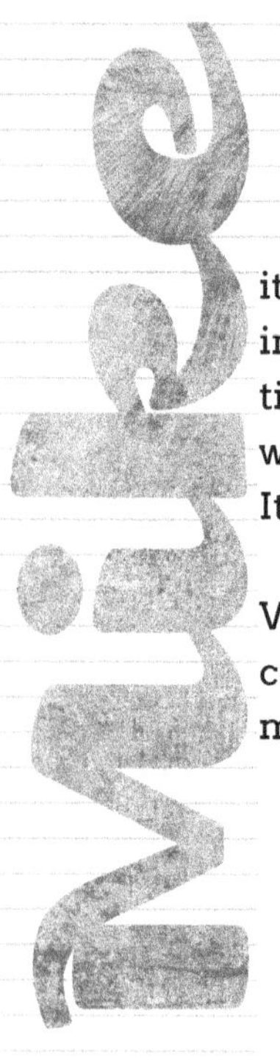

it. If I'd tried, I probably would've ended up accidentally shooting myself. I was in juvie for three months. It was hell, man. Everybody who goes to jail the first time, they bust out and cry. I cried in front of my mom. My older homies in juvie were like, "Man, you can't do that shit in here. You gotta swallow your emotions. It makes you weak, it makes you our prey." So it just kind of made me tougher.

When I got out of juvenile hall everybody started looking up to me. I was the coolest cat in the whole group because I'd done time. That time in juvie made me a predator instead of a prey. A big ol' gangster predator.

Making Connections

What is one thing you already know about immigration to the US?

I met my wife, Janet, in '94, when I was sixteen, and my son was born in '96. I was there at the hospital when he was born, and it was one of those feelings you never get in life, you know? A one-of-a-kind feeling. It was just amazing the way he looked. He was so cute and adorable. But just because you have a kid doesn't mean you're a father. You have to be around. I wasn't around. I was always on the streets or I was locked up. I went to jail like every six months. And shit, I didn't know nothing about being a dad. It just happened. I was a baby myself, and I was always on drugs, so having a baby didn't make a difference to me. I was so much into the gang life. I got more deep into it than I realized. I kid you not, my heart was into it, and I couldn't leave no more.

Santa Rita Prison

The whole time I was at Santa Rita and prison, I absorbed every bit of knowledge. You know how you go to school and you observe? Imagine not going to college, right? Instead, you choose to be a gangster. A dope dealer. You're in junior high at juvenile hall. You got this junior high knowledge and you graduate. You go to high school, right? From high school, now you graduate and go to college. Santa Rita was like college. And then your whole goal is to graduate from college. You get pointers on how to be a real gangster. How to be a real dope dealer. How to be a real hustler. How to do all the stuff you didn't think

30

Después de eso, mis *homeboys* y yo nos dedicamos a la vida de pandilleros.
Me metí en la vida de pandillas de los pies a la cabeza. Era lo más *cool* que se
podía hacer. Si eras un pandillero, eras el tipo más *cool* de la calle, de la escuela,
de todo. Fui por primera vez al centro de detención juvenil en 1992. Le apunté
con un arma a alguien en la escuela. Nos estábamos peleando y yo llevaba una
pistola que uno de mis *homeboys* me había dado. Pero no sabía cómo usarla. Si
hubiera intentado usarla, probablemente habría terminado disparándome a mí
mismo por accidente.

Estuve en detención juvenil durante tres meses. Híjole, eso fue un infierno.
Los que van a la cárcel por primera vez, se quiebran y lloran. Yo lloré delante
de mi mamá. Y mis *homies* más grandes, que estaban en la cárcel juvenil, me
decían, "No, hombre, no puedes hacer esa mierda aquí. Tienes que tragarte tus
emociones. Te hace ver débil, te convierte en nuestra presa". Así que eso me
hizo más rudo.

Cuando salí del centro de detención juvenil, todo el mundo empezó a admi-
rarme. Yo era el tipo más *cool* de todo el grupo porque había pasado tiempo
en la cárcel. Ese tiempo en la cárcel juvenil me convirtió en un depredador en
lugar de una presa. Yo era un gran pandillero depredador.

Conocí a mi esposa, Janet, en 1994, cuando yo tenía dieciséis años, y mi hijo
nació en 1996. Estuve en el hospital cuando nació, y fue una de esas emociones
tan únicas en la vida, ¿sabes? Es una sensación única. Era simplemente
increíble la forma en que mi hijo se veía. Era tan lindo y adorable. Pero el
hecho de que tengas un hijo no significa que tú seas un papá. Tienes que estar
presente. Yo no estaba presente. Siempre estaba en la calle o tras las rejas. Iba a
la cárcel como cada seis meses. Y, mierda, yo no sabía nada sobre cómo ser papá.
Pasó tan rápido. Yo mismo era un bebé y siempre estaba drogado, así que tener
un bebé no me importaba. Estaba tan metido en la vida de las pandillas. Me metí
más de lo que me di cuenta. No es broma, mi corazón estaba tan profundamente
metido en eso y no podía dejar esa vida atrás.

La Prisión De Santa Rita

Durante todo el tiempo que estuve en Santa Rita y en la prisión, yo absorbí cada
pedacito de conocimiento. Sabes, como vas a la escuela y observas, ¿cierto?
Ahora, imagina no ir a la universidad, ¿me entiendes? Y en lugar, eliges ser
un pandillero. Un traficante de drogas. Y vas a la secundaria del centro de
detención juvenil. Aprendés las cosas de secundaria y te gradúas. Vas al *high
school*, ¿verdad? Bueno, de *high school*, ahora te gradúas y vas a la universidad.
La prisión de Santa Rita era como la universidad. Y la meta aquí es graduarse de

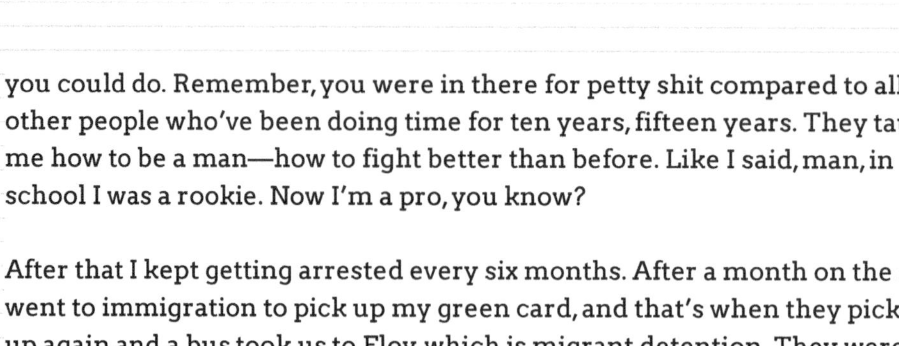

you could do. Remember, you were in there for petty shit compared to all the other people who've been doing time for ten years, fifteen years. They taught me how to be a man—how to fight better than before. Like I said, man, in high school I was a rookie. Now I'm a pro, you know?

After that I kept getting arrested every six months. After a month on the street, I went to immigration to pick up my green card, and that's when they picked me up again and a bus took us to Eloy, which is migrant detention. They were going to try to deport me.

Immigration said my crimes were deportable, so that's why they picked me up again. The drug cases are what sent me to immigration detention, even though I never got convicted for transporting, just possession. Immigration said I was transporting. So that's why I got sent to Eloy, to await deportation.

Eloy Immigration Detention

Eloy was loud. We were secluded from the world in a desert. There's sandstorms, and when we had to go to the cafeteria during a sandstorm, we'd walk outside and the sand would be so thick you couldn't see the guy in front of you. The sand and dust would come through the vent. We'd get spiders and scorpions in there. It was cold at night—we'd have to wear our beanies and jackets. The water was harsh—it was well water, and it tasted like chemicals. We'd melt ice down and drink that instead.

Making Connections

What is one thing you learned about immigrant detention in the US?

Going to prison and going to an immigration detention center are two different things. Prison is more structured. Immigration has all these people who come and go. In prison, you know your sentence, how long you've got left. But in immigration detention, they'll hold you until they can deport you. And that's for life. You're never coming back to this country again.

la universidad. Ahí recibes consejos sobre cómo ser un verdadero pandillero. Cómo ser un verdadero traficante de drogas. Cómo ser un verdadero estafador. Cómo hacer todas las cosas que no creías que podías hacer. Acuérdate que estabas ahí por tonterías en comparación con todas las demás personas que han estado cumpliendo condena durante diez años, quince años. Ellos me enseñaron a cómo ser un hombre, cómo pelear mejor que antes. Como te dije, amigo, en la *high school* yo era un novato. Ahora soy un *pro*, ¿me entiendes?

Después de eso, me arrestaban cada seis meses. Luego de un mes en la calle, fui a inmigración a recoger mi *green card*, y ahí fue cuando me volvieron a agarrar y un autobús nos llevó a Eloy, que es el centro de detención de migrantes. Iban a intentar deportarme.

La migra me dijo que mis delitos eran suficiente para deportarme, por eso me detuvieron de nuevo. Los casos de drogas son los que me enviaron a la detención de inmigrantes, aunque nunca me condenaron por tráfico, solo por posesión. La migra dijo que yo había estado traficando. Entonces por eso me enviaron a Eloy, a esperar mi deportación.

Centro De Detención Migratoria Eloy

Había mucho ruido en Eloy. Estábamos en el desierto, aislados del mundo. Hay tormentas de arena, y cuando teníamos que ir a la cafetería durante una tormenta de arena, salíamos y la arena era tan espesa que no podías ver al tipo al frente tuyo. La arena y el polvo entraban por el conducto de ventilación. Teníamos arañas y escorpiones ahí. Hacía frío por la noche, teníamos que usar nuestros gorros y chaquetas. El agua era pesada, era agua de pozo y sabía a productos químicos. Derretíamos hielo y bebíamos eso en su lugar.

Ir a prisión e ir a un centro de detención de inmigrantes son dos cosas diferentes. La prisión está más estructurada. El centro de detención tiene mucha gente que va y viene. En prisión, sabes tu sentencia, cuánto tiempo te queda. Pero en un centro de detención, te retendrán hasta que puedan deportar. Y eso es de por vida. Nunca más volverás a este país.

Regresar a Fiji puede sonar bien para algunas personas, pero acuérdate que irse de vacaciones y ser deportado son dos cosas diferentes, ¿cierto? Si vuelves con grilletes, es una historia completamente diferente. No recibirás el mismo respeto o trato. La gente en Fiji te vería como un criminal. Yo no quería volver. Decidí que pelearía mi caso todo el tiempo que me llevara. Además, hay muchas personas en Eloy que llegaron a los Estados Unidos tan jóvenes que crecieron pensando que eran ciudadanos estadounidenses. Yo pensé que yo

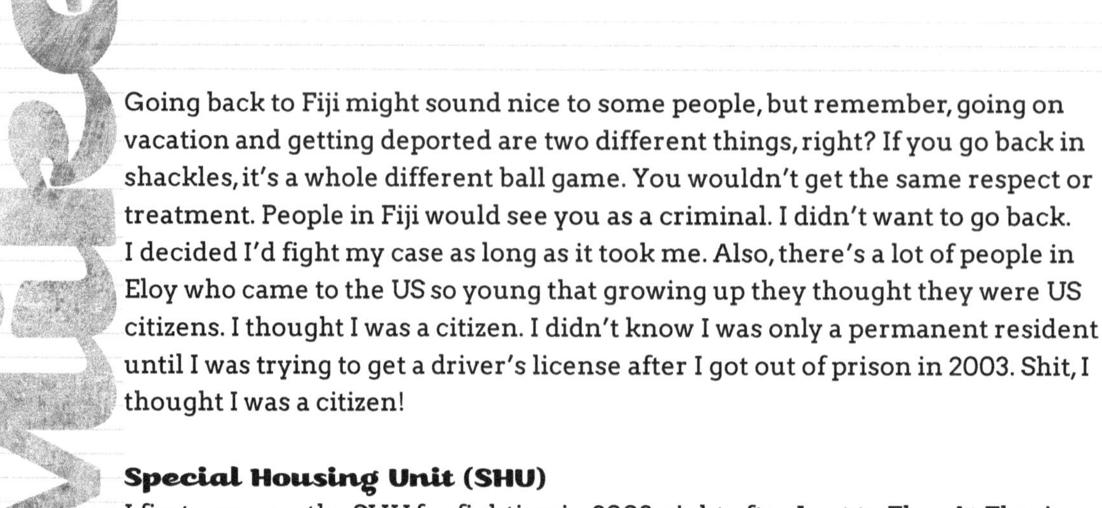

Going back to Fiji might sound nice to some people, but remember, going on vacation and getting deported are two different things, right? If you go back in shackles, it's a whole different ball game. You wouldn't get the same respect or treatment. People in Fiji would see you as a criminal. I didn't want to go back. I decided I'd fight my case as long as it took me. Also, there's a lot of people in Eloy who came to the US so young that growing up they thought they were US citizens. I thought I was a citizen. I didn't know I was only a permanent resident until I was trying to get a driver's license after I got out of prison in 2003. Shit, I thought I was a citizen!

Special Housing Unit (SHU)

I first came on the SHU for fighting in 2003, right after I got to Eloy. At Eloy in the SHU, they got you alone in a cell. And you got to learn to live with this now. You're confined in a six-by-nine cell with a solid steel door that has a metal screen in it so the guards could look inside and see what you're doing. You get three meals a day. You get yard for one hour three times a week, then a shower. Every time you move you gotta get shackled up.

In order to survive, you gotta structure yourself. Gotta get up, work out, take a shower. Pray. Eat. You gotta get a couple of good books, you gotta read books, you gotta keep yourself busy. Soon as you're thinking, *Aw, man. Shit, I ain't got nothing to do.* Now your mind's wondering, *What's going on in the streets?* Now your mind's wondering what's your wife doing. Now your mind's wondering how's your kid doing, how's your mom and dad doing, right? Soon as you start thinking more, you start stressing. As soon as you start stressing more, you start tripping out more. So then you start tripping out more, now the walls are tripping on you, right? You start getting delusional. You start seeing all this shit that's not there, because your mind's fucking running wild.

Stop To Think...

Write three words that describe how you feel reading Mike's story so far.

This happened to me, but thank God I got it under control. But it happened. Being in the SHU is like being a dog tied to a pole with a ten-foot chain.

era ciudadano. No sabía que solo era residente permanente hasta que traté de conseguir una licencia de conducir después de salir de prisión en 2003. Mierda, ¡pensé que era un ciudadano!

Unidad De Vivienda Especial (SHU, Por Sus Siglas En Inglés)

Entré por primera vez a la SHU por pelear en 2003, justo después de llegar a Eloy. En la SHU de Eloy, te tienen solo, en una celda. Y tienes que aprender a vivir así. Estás confinado en una celda de 2 x 3 metros con una puerta de acero sólido que tiene una malla de metal para que los guardias puedan mirar dentro y ver lo que estás haciendo. Te dan de comer tres veces al día. Puedes salir al patio una hora tres veces a la semana, y luego una ducha. Cada vez que vas a otro lugar tienes que estar encadenado.

Para sobrevivir, tienes que estructurar tu tiempo. Tienes que levantarte, hacer ejercicio, darte una ducha. Orar. Comer. Tienes que conseguir un par de buenos libros, tienes que leer libros, tienes que mantenerte ocupado. Tan pronto como estés pensando, "Ayy, hombre. Mierda, no tengo nada que hacer". Ahí, tu mente comienza a preguntarse, *¿Qué estará pasando en las calles?* Y luego, *¿Qué está haciendo mi esposa?* o *¿Cómo le va a mi hijo?*, *¿Cómo le va a mi mamá?* y *¿a mi papá?*, ¿verdad? Tan pronto como empiezas a pensar más, empiezas a estresarte. Tan pronto como comienzas a estresarte más, tu mente comienza a divagar. Entonces te empiezas a perder más y las paredes comienzan a dar vuelta, ¿verdad? Y empiezas a delirar. Y comienzas a ver toda esta mierda que no está ahí, pero es porque tu mente se está volviendo loca.

Eso me pasó a mí, pero gracias a Dios pude controlarlo. Pero me sucedió. Estar en la SHU es como ser un perro atado a un poste con una cadena de tres metros de largo. Imagina dejar a un perro así durante meses seguidos. El perro puede comer, beber, cagar, ducharse y todo eso, pero solo ahí en ese espacio de tres metros. No puede irse a ningún otro lado más que esos tres metros, ¿me entiendes? Imagínate por lo que está pasando. Durante treinta días, y luego dos meses. Ocho meses. Diez meses. Imagínate.

Mucha gente murió en la SHU. La atención médica era terrible. Conocí a un hombre de Fiji que tenía la presión alta y no lo atendieron y tuvo un infarto. Había personas con enfermedades mentales que no estaban recibiendo sus medicamentos. Vi a dos personas perder por completo la cabeza y volverse locos ahí. Solo se volvieron locos, ¡hombre! Si no tienes una mente fuerte y no tienes una voluntad fuerte, estás jodido.

Imagine leaving a dog like that for months at a time. He could eat, drink, shit, you know, take a shower and everything, but just in that space right there, ten feet. He can't go anywhere besides that ten feet, you know? Imagine what he's going through. For thirty days, two months. Eight months. Ten months. Imagine.

A lot of people died in the SHU. The medical attention was horrible. One Fijian guy I knew had high blood pressure and it wasn't treated, and he had a heart attack. There were mentally ill people who weren't medicated. I saw two people straight up lose their minds in there and go crazy. They fucking just lost it, dude. If you're not strong-minded, and you don't have that strong will, you're screwed.

Three days a week you get to leave your cell. And what I remember most was how it enrages you. It's like being a kid and you look out the window and see everybody playing and having fun, and you can't join them for some reason. You start to get angrier and angrier, and you have all this hate for everybody. If you don't know how to release it, when you finally do come out, you come out angrier than before.

Still, some things I actually liked better about being in SHU. I got to read a lot of books. I got to actually read the Quran and understand it. I got to freakin' have the peace of mind to think, work out, you know? But after a while it got to me. We have to act all tough and put up this front, but I got wore out. I just thought, Send me back to Fiji, I can't take it anymore.

In 2003 I got connected with the Florence Project, which helps with legal cases in immigration centers all over the area. The Florence Project comes into Eloy to do pro bono work, so that's how I met my two lawyers, Rachel and Holly. They encouraged me to fight my case.

I'd just about given up fighting, but I remember what changed things for me was that I broke down and cried in front of my lawyer, Rachel. I think that was the biggest thing—when I broke down crying in front of her. It took a burden off my chest. I think that changed me. It just—like all the pain and stuff you hold inside, it broke. I broke down and cried like crazy. And I think that helped. I started growing after that. I wasn't thinking about going back to the streets and all my grudges anymore, I just wanted to go home.

I was freed September 27, 2007. I was still under threat of deportation until 2010, but we fought and had my convictions dropped. And after that, there was no threat of deportation.

Puedes salir de tu celda tres días a la semana. Y lo que más recuerdo es cómo te enfurece. Es como ser un niño y mirar por la ventana y ver a todos los demás jugando y divirtiéndose, y por alguna razón no puedes jugar con ellos. Empiezas a enojarte más y más, y sientes todo ese odio por todos. Si no sabes cómo soltarlo, cuando finalmente sales, sales más enojado que antes.

Y aún así, hubo algunas cosas que sí me gustaron de estar en la SHU. Tuve la oportunidad de leer muchos libros. Pude leer el Corán y entenderlo. Pude por fin tener paz de mente para pensar, hacer ejercicio, ¿sabes? Pero después de un tiempo me afectó. Teníamos que actuar fuertes y aguantarnos, pero me cansé. Solo pensaba, "Mándame de regreso a Fiji, ya no aguanto más".

En 2003 me conectaron con el Florence Project, que ayuda con casos legales en centros de inmigración en toda la zona. El Florence Project va a Eloy para hacer trabajo pro bono, así es como conocí a mis dos abogadas, Rachel y Holly. Me animaron a pelear mi caso.

Casi me había dado por vencido, pero recuerdo que lo que cambió las cosas para mí fue que me derrumbé y lloré frente a mi abogada, Rachel. Creo que eso fue lo más importante, cuando rompí a llorar frente a ella. Me quitó un peso de encima. Creo que eso me cambió. Es que todo el dolor y las cosas que tenía dentro, las saqué. Me derrumbé y lloré como loco. Y creo que eso me ayudó. Comencé a crecer después de eso. Ya no pensaba en volver a las calles y en todos mis rencores, solo quería irme a casa.

Me liberaron el 27 de septiembre de 2007. Todavía estaba bajo amenaza de deportación hasta el 2010, pero luchamos y mis condenas fueron anuladas. Y después de eso, no hubo amenaza de deportación.

La Vida Después De La Prisión

En el 2007, salí de la SHU directo a la calle. Al principio fue un poco extraño estar libre. De 1992 a 2007, todo lo que hice fue que me encerraran o me dispararan. Nunca tuve un trabajo de verdad ni nada.

Mi hermano está encerrado de por vida, ¿cierto? Mi papá y yo obtuvimos la custodia de sus cuatro hijos. Así que ahora tengo cuatro adolescentes a cargo. Solo somos yo, mi papá y mi hermana cuidándolos. Mi hermana y su esposo tienen cinco hijos, así que somos trece personas en la casa de mi hermana con cuatro habitaciones. Lo estamos resolviendo, pero a veces me siento muy, muy perdido.

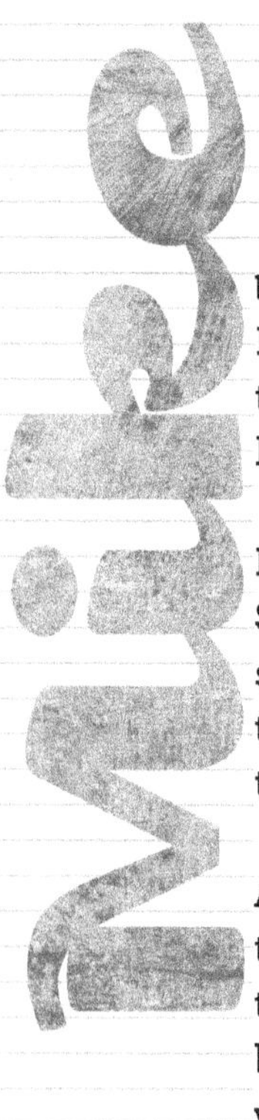

Life After Prison

In 2007, I came from the SHU straight out to the street. At first it was a little trippy being out. From 1992 to 2007, all I did was get locked up or shot. I never had a real job or nothing.

My brother's locked up for life, right? My dad and I got custody of his four kids. So now I have four teenagers on my hands. It's just me and my dad and my sister looking after them. My sister and her husband have five kids, so there's thirteen of us in my sister's four-bedroom house. We're making do, but sometimes I feel really, really lost.

At home I'm struggling. When you're in isolation, you get this peace of mind that you're safe because nobody can get to you, nobody can hurt you. I miss that shit. It's fucked up because I don't want to go back to jail, but my responsibilities are overwhelming. There's so much shit on my plate with the kids and work. Lately I'm trying to distance myself from the world. I don't know why. Usually I'm a really social guy, but lately I'm isolating myself. It's flashbacks from jail. I got so used to being isolated from everything. So now I isolate myself from people. All I know is SHU. This shit is really getting to me, but I don't want to show my family because they're all depending on me.

Stop To Think...

Highlight three parts of the story that describe how Mike is feeling after returning home from prison.

In my room I'm just thinking most of the time. Thinking, like *Damn, I wasted most of my life doing stupid shit and getting locked up.* All I did was party and try to be a gangster. Try to live that American dream to be a fuckin' gangster. If I could change the past, I would do a lot of shit different. But you can't. You can't go back.

I'm trying, I don't do anything wrong. I don't drink, I don't get mad, but when I was bad everything was cool. But now I'm struggling. If you hustle, you make more money than working. Do you know how easy it is to be bad? Do you know how hard it is to be good? I go to work every day and work overtime and I still

Es difícil estar en casa. Cuando estás aislado, tienes la tranquilidad de saber que estás a salvo porque nadie puede llegar a ti, nadie puede lastimarte. Extraño esa mierda. Está jodido porque no quiero volver a la cárcel, pero mis responsabilidades son abrumadoras. Tengo tantas cosas que hacer con los chicos y el trabajo. Últimamente intento distanciarme del mundo. No sé por qué. Por lo general, soy una persona muy sociable, pero últimamente me estoy aislando. Son recuerdos de estar en la cárcel. Me acostumbré tanto a estar aislado de todo. Así que ahora me aíslo de la gente. Todo lo que conozco es estar en la SHU. Esa mierda de verdad me está afectando, pero no quiero mostrárselo a mi familia porque todos dependen de mí.

Cuando estoy en mi cuarto, me paso la mayor parte del tiempo pensando. Pensando, *¡maldita sea!, desperdicié la mayor parte de mi vida haciendo estupideces y encarcelado.* Todo lo que hacía era hacer fiesta e intentar ser un pandillero. Intentar vivir ese sueño americano de ser un maldito pandillero. Si pudiera cambiar el pasado, haría muchas cosas diferentes. Pero no se puede. No se puede regresar al pasado.

Lo estoy intentando, y ahora no hago nada malo. No tomo, no me enojo, pero cuando yo era malo todo iba bien. Pero ahora me cuesta. Si vendes drogas, ganas más dinero que cuando trabajas. ¿Sabes lo fácil que es ser malo? ¿Sabes lo difícil que es ser bueno? Salgo a trabajar todos los días y hago horas extras y aún así apenas salgo adelante. Trabajo en el hospital Mills Peninsula. Soy del personal de aseo. Recojo la ropa de cama y la basura. Me gusta mi trabajo, puedo conocer a gente y siento que hago una diferencia porque trabajo en un hospital. Hay muchas cosas buenas, pero hay gente que no te habla debido al trabajo que haces. La gente te desprecia cuando recoges basura y limpias suelos y baños.

Tuve una segunda oportunidad, pero es una segunda oportunidad jodida. No estoy en una celda, pero estoy atrapado con las responsabilidades y mi trabajo. El hijo mayor de mi hermano acaba de empezar la universidad. Quiere ser abogado. Les dije a los hijos de mi hermano: "Sólo tienen una oportunidad en la vida. Sólo una. No sean como yo, que comencé a vivir a los treinta y sigo tratando de recuperar el tiempo perdido".

Así que les di a elegir: "Van a ser buenos o malos. ¿Qué van a elegir?" No puedes estar en el medio. No puedes ser ambos. Si eres malo, dale con todo y sé malo. Y no puedo hacer nada sobre eso más que respetarte, porque yo también hice eso. Pero si quieres ser bueno, dale con todo y sé bueno. No puedes ser ambos. Y son buenos.

barely get by. I work at Mills Peninsula hospital. I'm a housekeeper. I pick up linen and trash. I like my job, I get to meet people, and I actually feel like I make a difference because it's a hospital. There's a lot of positives, but some people won't talk to you because of your job. People look down on you when you pick up garbage, clean floors, toilets.

Interview Skills

What is one thing you would want to ask Mike about his time in immigrant detention?

I got a second chance, but it's a fucked-up second chance. I'm free from a cell, but I'm locked up with responsibilities and my job. The oldest of my brother's kids, he just started university. He wants to be a lawyer. I told my brother's kids, "You only get one chance in life. That's it. Don't be like me, starting life at thirty, still catching up on life."

So I gave them a choice: either you're gonna be good or bad. Which one is it? You can't be in the middle. You can't do both. If you're bad, then go all out and be bad. And I can't do nothing but respect you because I did it. But if you wanna be good, go all out and be good. You can't do both. So they're good.

Storyboard

In each of the four boxes below, draw a picture that represents an important part of Mike's journey. Use labels, captions, and/or speech bubbles to help you capture who is in your drawing, what is happening, and where it takes place. Use colors and symbols to help you capture how each person is feeling in that moment. Don't worry if you don't consider yourself to be a great artist–just try your best!

Use an excerpt from Mike's story to create your own blackout poem! Pick out the most important words and phrases in the excerpt, then use a marker to black out everything else. Use the words that are left over to create a poem: you can change the order of the words, and add line breaks or punctuation wherever you want. The only trick is that you cannot add any new words!

Excerpt:

I'd just about given up fighting, but I remember what changed things for me was that I broke down and cried in front of my lawyer, Rachel. I think that was the biggest thing—when I broke down crying in front of her. It took a burden off my chest. I think that changed me. It just—like all the pain and stuff you hold inside, it broke. I broke down and cried like crazy. And I think that helped. I started growing after that. I wasn't thinking about going back to the streets and all my grudges anymore, I just wanted to go home.

With Blackouts:

Finished Poem:

Given up fighting,
What changed?
I broke down, I think
Crying changed me.
All the pain broke down.
That helped:
Growing,
Going home.

Excerpt:

I'm trying, I don't do anything wrong. I don't drink, I don't get mad but when I was bad everything was cool. But now I'm struggling. If you hustle, you make more money than working. Do you know how easy it is to be bad? Do you know how hard it is to be good? I go to work every day and work overtime and I still barely get by. I work at Mills Peninsula hospital. I'm a housekeeper. I pick up linen and trash. I like my job, I get to meet people, and I actually feel like I make a difference because it's a hospital. There's a lot of positives, but some people won't talk to you because of your job. People look down on you when you pick up garbage, clean floors, toilets. I'm free from a cell, but I'm locked up with responsibilities and my job. The oldest of my brother's kids, he just started university. He wants to be a lawyer. I told my brother's kids, "You only get one chance in life. That's it. Don't be like me, starting life at thirty, still catching up on life."

Finished Poem:

If you had a chance to write a letter to Mike, what would you want to say? In the space provided, write a letter addressed to Mike about your response to his story. You can ask questions, make personal connections to your own experiences, talk about what his story has taught you, express gratitude or admiration—whatever feels most important to you! Make sure to reference at least two specific details from Mike's story in your letter.

Spend some time thinking about each of the following questions. Use the boxes provided to jot down your thoughts and to collect evidence to support your answers. Then, you will use your notes to participate in a class discussion on these questions.

Why is it hard for Mike to escape the cycle of going to prison and getting released in his younger years?

❯ Your Response:

❯ Evidence:

How is immigrant detention different from prison? In what ways is it similar?

❯ Your Response:

❯ Evidence:

What are the physical, mental, and emotional effects of being in solitary confinement (SHU)?

❯ Your Response:

❯ Evidence:

What is life like for Mike after returning home from prison?

❯ Your Response:

❯ Evidence:

What types of support do you think should be available for formerly incarcerated people?

❯ Your Response:

Do you think that our current prison system is a fair way to address crime? Why or why not? In your opinion, what would 'criminal justice' look like?

❯ Your Response:

Audio Recordings

Audio recordings of each narrative in both English and Spanish can be found on the Voice of Witness website.

Classroom Resources

Along with the activities embedded inside this workbook, please visit the Voice of Witness website for more lesson plans. These narratives can be used alongside an Ethnic Studies framework and as a launchpad for an independent oral history unit.

www.voiceofwitness.org/workbook-1

www.ingramcontent.com/pod-product-compliance
Lightning Source LLC
Chambersburg PA
CBHW041837110726
48006CB00020B/2655